JOHN RUTTER

WINCHESTER TE DEUM

FOR MIXED VOICES AND ORGAN,
ORGAN WITH BRASS ENSEMBLE,
OR ORCHESTRA

T0056053

MUSIC DEPARTMENT

OXFORD
UNIVERSITY PRESS

OXFORD
UNIVERSITY PRESS

Great Clarendon Street, Oxford OX2 6DP, England
198 Madison Avenue, New York, NY 10016, USA

Oxford University Press is a department of the University of Oxford.
It furthers the University's aim of excellence in research, scholarship,
and education by publishing worldwide in

Oxford New York
Auckland Cape Town Hong Kong Karachi
Kuala Lumpur Madrid Melbourne Mexico City Nairobi
New Delhi Shanghai Taipei Toronto

With offices in

Argentina Austria Brazil Chile Czech Republic France Greece
Guatemala Hungary Italy Japan Poland Portugal Singapore
South Korea Switzerland Thailand Turkey Ukraine Vietnam

Oxford is a registered trade mark of Oxford University Press
in the UK and in certain other countries

© Collegium Music Publications 2006
Exclusively licensed to Oxford University Press

John Rutter has asserted his right under the Copyright, Designs
and Patents Act, 1988, to be identified as Composer of this Work

Database right Oxford University Press (maker)

First published 2007

All rights reserved. No part of this publication may be reproduced,
stored in a retrieval system, or transmitted, in any form or by any means,
without the prior permission in writing of Oxford University Press,
or as expressly permitted by law. Enquiries concerning reproduction
outside the scope of the above should be sent to the Music Copyright
Department, Oxford University Press, at the address above

Permission to perform this work in public
(except in the course of divine worship) should normally be obtained
from the Performing Right Society Ltd. (PRS), 29/33 Berners Street,
London W1T 3AB, or its affiliated Societies in each country throughout
the world, unless the owner or the occupier of the premises
being used holds a licence from the Society

Permission to make a recording must be obtained in advance
from the Mechanical-Copyright Protection Society Ltd. (MCPS),
Elgar House, 41 Streatham High Road, London SW16 1ER,
or its affiliated Societies in each country throughout the world

10

ISBN 978-0-19-335689-4

Printed in Great Britain on acid-free paper by
Halstan & Co. Ltd., Amersham, Bucks.

INSTRUMENTATION

The accompaniment to this work exists in three versions:

1. For organ alone. The organist plays from the vocal score.

2. For organ with five-part brass ensemble (2 trumpets in B flat, horn in F, trombone, and tuba), plus optional timpani (1 player) and optional percussion (2 players). The organist plays from the full score.

3. For full orchestra (without organ).

Full scores and instrumental parts for versions 2 and 3 are available on hire from the publisher. Please specify, when ordering, which version is required.

Duration: 7–8 minutes

for Winchester Cathedral, on the occasion of
the installation of the Very Reverend James Atwell as Dean,
25th March 2006

Winchester Te Deum

JOHN RUTTER

© Collegium Music Publications 2006. Exclusively licensed to Oxford University Press. The Moral Rights of the Composer have been asserted.

31
thee: the Fa - ther ev - er - last - ing, the Fa - - - ther ev - er -
Sw.
41
B
-last - ing.
Gt. or Ch.
B
f
dim.
51
SOPRANOS
f
C
(Sops. div.)
To thee all an - gels cry a - loud: the hea - vens, the
ALTOS
f
To thee all an - gels cry a - loud: the
C
mf
Ch.

59
D
1
S.
2
A.
hea - vens and all the Pow - ers there - in. To thee Che -
hea - vens and all the Pow - ers there - in. To thee Che -
hea - vens and all the Pow - ers there - in. To thee Che -
D
Sw.
legato

66
- ru-bin and Se-ra-phin: con - tin - ual - ly do
- ru-bin and Se-ra-phin: con - tin - ual - ly do cry, con -
- ru-bin and Se-ra-phin: con - tin - ual - ly do cry, con -

73
E
mp
cry, con - tin - ual - ly do cry, Ho - ly,
mp
- tin - ual - ly do cry, Ho - ly, Ho - ly,
mp
- tin - ual - ly do cry, Ho - ly, Ho - ly, Ho - ly,
E
Ch. with mutations
p
83
Ho - ly, Ho - ly: Lord God of Sa-ba-oth;
Ho - ly, Ho - ly, Ho - ly: Lord God of Sa-ba-oth;
Ho - ly, Ho - ly, Ho - ly: Lord God of Sa-ba-oth;
cresc.

94
TENORS
F
f
Hea - ven and earth are full of the Ma - je - sty of thy
BASSES
f
Hea - ven and earth are full of the Ma - je - sty of thy
Gt.
F
mf legato
101
Same beat ♩ = 80
Glo - ry, of thy Glo - ry.
Glo - ry, of thy Glo - ry.
Solo Tpt.
2
2
Same beat ♩ = 80
108
SOPRANO
ff cantabile
G
poco a poco accelerando
ALTO
The glo - ri - ous com - pa - ny of the A - pos - tles praise thee,
TENOR
The
BASS
ff cantabile
glo - ri - ous com - pa - ny
f
Gt.
G
poco a poco accelerando
f
Gt.
mf

112
(accel. sempre)
mf
The no - ble ar - my of Mar - tyrs praise_
good - ly fel - low-ship of the Pro - phets praise thee.
mf
(accel. sempre)
mp
Andante con moto ♩ = 96
H
116
thee.
The ho - ly Church through-out all the world doth ac -
mp
Andante con moto ♩ = 96
H
Sw.
mp
p
legato
Sw.

119
mp
-know - ledge thee; The Fa - ther of an in - - fi - nite Ma - je - sty, Thine
Solo Fl.
123
p dolce
Al - so the Ho - ly Ghost, the
hon - our - a - ble, true, and on - ly Son;
Sw.
Fl.
dim.
pp dolce e legato

128
Com - fort - er.
pp
the Com - fort - er.
pp
I
accelerando
Lento ♩ = 48 = 𝅗𝅥 of preceding
Gt.
Ch. or Solo
mp
cresc. poco a poco
Gt.
(accel.)
133
J Andante maestoso ♩ = 80
ff
Thou art the King of glo - ry, O Christ.
ff
(accel.)
J Andante maestoso ♩ = 80
Solo Tpt.
f
f
Gt.

140
f
Thou art the ev - er - last - ing Son of the Fa - ther.
f
Gt.
Tpt.
145
mf
K
p
When thou took - est up - on thee to de - liv - er man: thou didst not ab - hor the Vir - gin's
mf
p
mf
Sw.
K
legato
p
mf
Sw.
149
mp
cresc.
mf
womb. When thou hadst ov - er - come the sharp - ness of death: thou didst op - en the
mp
cresc.
mf
mp
cresc.
mf

153
accelerando
King - dom of hea - ven to all be - liev - ers.
accelerando
Gt.
Gt.
f
157
L Con moto ♩ = 96
ff
f
Thou sit - test at the right hand of God: in the glo - ry of the
ff
f
in the
L Con moto ♩ = 96
ff
162
p pesante
rall.
Fa - ther. We be - lieve that thou shalt come: to be our
p pesante
rall.
Sw. p

Lento ♩ = 48 = 𝅗𝅥 of preceding
a tempo
167
SOPS div.
or S. & A.
mp
M
Judge.
We there-fore pray thee, help thy ser-vants: whom thou hast re-
Lento ♩ = 48 = 𝅗𝅥 of preceding
a tempo
Ch. Fl.
p
Ch. Fl.
172
N poco a poco accel.
S.
mp
-deem-ed with thy pre-cious blood.
A.
Make them to be
T.
B.
mp
N poco a poco accel.
Sw.
mp
Sw.
177
mp cresc.
mf
num-bered with thy Saints: In glo-ry ev-er-last-ing, in
mp cresc.
mf
cresc.
mf

181
cresc.
Maestoso ♩ = 80
f
cresc.
ff
glo - ry ev - er - last - ing, in glo - ry ev - er - last - ing.
glo - ry
cresc.
f
cresc.
ff
Maestoso ♩ = 80
cresc.
f
Gt.
Gt.
O
185
ff largamente e cantabile
f
189
dim.
mf dim.
mp dim.
p
Sw. (strings)
P
Ch.
p legato e quasi lontano

195
SOPRANOS
p
O Lord, save thy peo - ple:
Sw.
8 ft. only
202
mp
and bless thine he - ri - tage.
Go-vern them:
and lift them up for
207
mf
ev - er.
Q
TENORS
mp dolce
Day by day we mag-ni - fy thee;
mf
And we
mp
p
mp
+16 ft.

SOPRANOS
213
mp
wor - ship thy Name: ev - er world with - out end, ev - er
p
219
world with - out end.
R
S.
pp dolce
A.
Vouch - safe, O Lord:
T.
B.
pp dolce
R
pp
p
225
p
to keep us this day with - out sin.
O Lord, have mer - cy up -
p

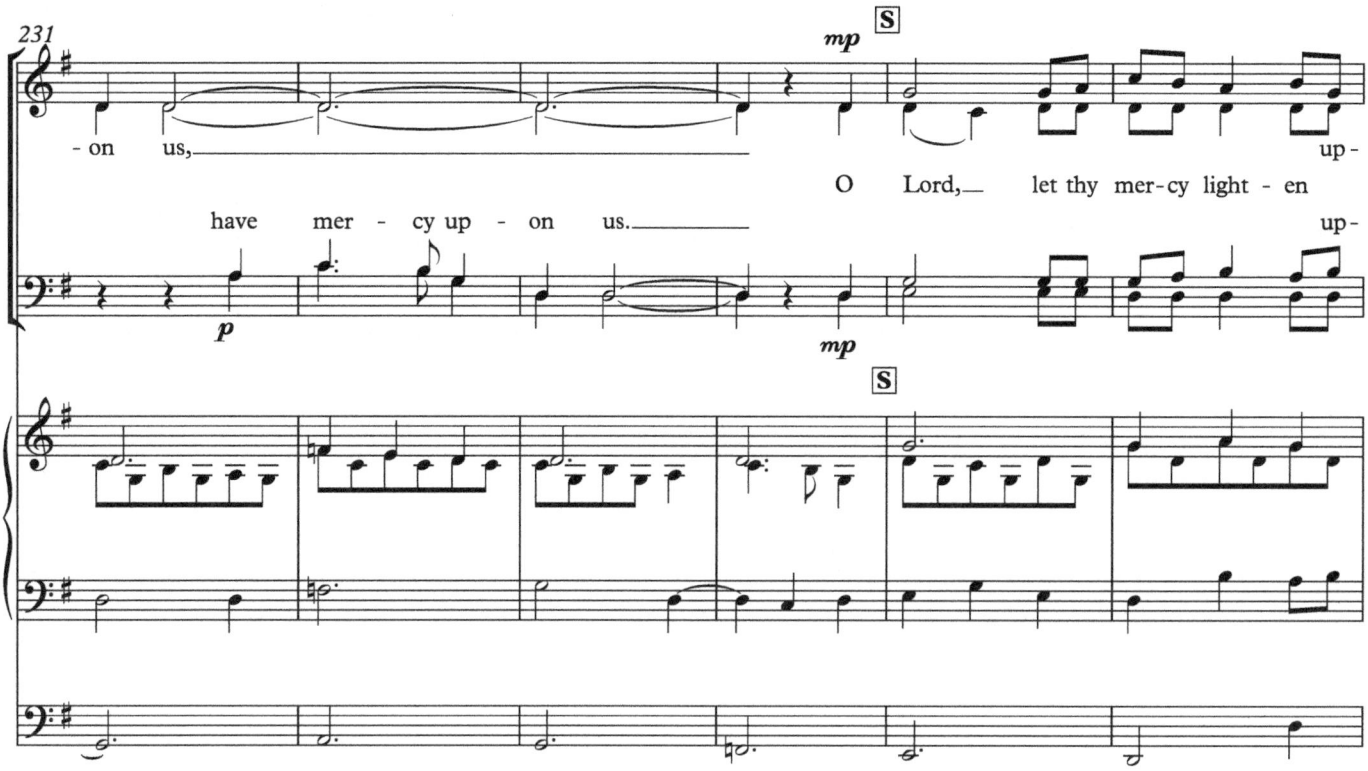
231
mp
S
- on us,
up-
O Lord, let thy mer-cy light - en
have mer - cy up - on us.
up-
p
mp
S

237
cresc.
mf
f
mf
-on us:
As our trust is in thee,
as our trust is in
As our trust, as our trust is in thee,
-on us:
cresc.
mf
trust is in thee,
mf
f
mp
mf
mp

243
dim.
p
thee,
thee, as our trust is in thee, as our trust is in
mp
p
p
pp
Quasi senza misura ♩ = c. 108
rit.
Tempo giusto
249
pp
T
mf cresc. molto
ff
S.
thee.
let me nev - er be con - found - ed.
pp
mf
cresc. molto
ff
A.
thee. O Lord, in thee have I trust - ed: let me nev - er be con - found - ed.
pp
cresc.
mp cresc.
f
T.
thee.
Lord,
Lord.
pp
cresc.
mp cresc.
f
B.
thee.
Lord,
Lord.
Quasi senza misura ♩ = c. 108
rit.
Tempo giusto
T

♩ = 80
Giubiloso ♩. = 80
U
255
Gt.
Sw.
f
ff
264
f ritmico e marcato
Al - le - lu - ia, al - le - lu - ia, al - le - lu -
Al - le - lu - ia, al - le - lu - ia, al - le - lu -
Al - le - lu - ia, al - le - lu -
Al - le - lu - ia, al - le - lu -

273
V
- ia, al - le - lu - ia, al - le - lu -
- ia, al - le - lu - ia,
- ia, al - le - lu - ia, al - le - lu -
- ia, al - le - lu - ia,
V
282
- ia, al - le - lu - ia, al - le - lu - ia,
al - le - lu - ia, al - le - lu - ia,
- ia, al - le - lu - ia, al - le - lu - ia,
al - le - lu - ia, al - le - lu - ia,

290
W
cresc.
ff
al - le - lu - ia, al - le - lu -
al - le - lu - ia, al - le - lu -
al - le - lu - ia, al - le - lu -
al - le - lu - ia,
298
f
- ia, al - le - lu - ia, al - le - lu - ia, al - le - lu -
- ia, al - le - lu - ia, al - le - lu - ia, al - le - lu -
- ia, al - le - lu - ia, al - le - lu - ia,
al - le - lu - ia, al - le - lu - ia,
mf

306
X
cresc.
ff
-ia, al - le - lu - ia, al - le - lu - ia,
f
al - le - lu - ia, al - le - lu - ia,
Solo Tba.
allargando al fine
314
fff
al - le - lu - ia.
Gt.